Protecting Your Retirement Income:

Four Techniques to Help Secure Your Retirement Income

Nelson R Beck

Disclaimer

I am not a licensed broker or an attorney or a tax advisor, or an accountant. I am not a financial planner. The information that you read here is for information and entertainment only. It is up to you to read, do your research, and make your own decisions. Remember, this is your retirement money, and no one cares more about your retirement money than you.

Any investments mentioned here are for your information only. I am not a licensed broker and am not selling any investments. Past performance is no guarantee of future results. Any investment listed here is not an offer to sell or a solicitation of an offer to buy.

Note to international readers: The calculations shown in these pages are applicable around the world. However, the retirement plans and investments discussed here are the types available in the United States. Therefore, consult your financial advisors, retirement planners, accountants, tax advisors, and attorneys as to the retirement plans and investments available in your country and the applicability of these investments for your retirement income. I make no guarantee or warranty as to the specific retirement plans or investments available around the world.

Author's Note

Nelson R. Beck was born in Cincinnati, Ohio. He received his BA and MA in history from the University of Cincinnati and MS in library science from the University of Illinois at Urbana-Champaign. He was a financial planner with IDS, American Express Financial Advisors and Ameriprise Financial from 1979 to 2011. He retired in 2011 and has practiced reflexology since 2011. He lives in Urbana, Illinois, with his wife Sherry. He enjoys reading, writing, and rail travel.

Table of Contents

INTRODUCTION

I worked as a financial planner for 32 years. In that time, I helped many individuals and couples with retirement planning. Although I retired from that business in 2011, I continue to read many articles and books about financial planning in general and retirement planning in particular.

As I read about retirement planning and income, several issues stand out. First, most of the writing falls into three categories. There are many books and articles about the tax and technical matters of retirement plans. Most of these writings are aimed at financial advisors and planners, accountants, and other professionals.

The second category is articles about retirement plans as they affect high-income and high-net-worth retirees. Much of this writing warns readers about large accumulations in retirement plans and the resulting tax bill on required minimum distributions.

The third area of writing concerns Social Security. Since 40% of retirees in the United States rely entirely on Social Security, this is certainly a vital area for investors and retirees to study.

Throughout these books and articles, there is a scarcity of discussion of the low retirement plan accumulation and the best ways to take an income, try to meet monthly living expenses, and make the money last throughout retirement.

In this book, I hope to offer several ideas for establishing retirement income for the middle-income retirees, for those with smaller balances in their 401(k) and other defined-contribution plans.

RETIREMENT PLANS THEN AND NOW

During the last half of the Twentieth Century, the predominant type of retirement plan was the defined benefit pension plan. Today, the majority of plans are defined-contribution plans. Of these, the 401(k) plan is widely offered to employees of corporations. The 401(k) is also available to small businesses and other sole proprietors. Additional defined contribution plans are the IRA, the Roth IRA, the Simple IRA, and, for the employees of schools, colleges, hospitals, museums, and other non-profit institutions, the 403(b) plan.

THE DEFINED BENEFIT PENSION PLAN

Offered by corporations in the last decades of the Twentieth Century, the defined benefit pension plan paid a guaranteed monthly income to retirees. This payment was based on the highest income or the average earnings of the employee. With the passage of the ERISA Act of 1974, pensions offered survivor benefits to the surviving spouse.

Some plans also provided a cost-of-living adjustment.

Defined benefit plans provided great comfort to millions of retirees but were very expensive to maintain. Contributions to the plan each year were made by the employer. To calculate the required contribution, it was the job of the employer to hire accountants and actuaries. Based upon the employee's income, age, account balance, assumed rate of return, and projected retirement age, the actuaries and accountants calculated the required contribution from the employer. This was obviously a very expensive endeavor. As a result, by the early 1980's employers began moving away from defined benefit pension plans and substituting them with defined contribution plans. The most common of these among corporations is the 401(k) plan.

Today, defined benefit pension plans are offered primarily by the Federal and state governments.

RETIREMENT PLAN TODAY

The defined contribution plan predominates today. Though IRAs, Roth IRAs, SIMPLE IRAs, and 403(b) plans are all very important and are defined-contribution plans, the type of plan most often available through the corporate employer is the 401(k) plan. As opposed to the defined benefit plan, the contributions to the 401(k) plans are made by employees. After an employee selects a percentage of income to contribute, the employer makes a matching contribution.

The contribution limits are set out in the tax law and the IRS Code. I will not delve into the contribution limits for 401(k) plans or other defined contribution plans. There are many books and articles that deal with these limits and regulations. There are also IRS publications that you can consult. Of course, you should talk to your accountant or attorney and other tax advisors, as well as your employer's human resources person or whoever handles your 401(k).

My purpose in writing this book is to help you explore ways of taking out a retirement income. Unlike the defined benefit pension, where the payout was/ is calculated by the employer, with the 401(k) plan and other defined contribution plans, making retirement income calculations and planning a payout is up to you.

I want to note here that the income methods described here can be applied to investments outside of retirement plans. Money in mutual funds, stocks, certificates of deposit, cash, and bonds can be used to provide the following methods of monthly or quarterly income.

So, what to do, what to do? In the following pages, I will describe four means of receiving monthly or quarterly retirement income. You can divide your money among all four techniques or use one method alone. In the interest of long-term diversification and safety of principal and income, it is best to divide your money among two or three of these ideas.

While a payout might be possible from a 401(k), it is best to roll over your 401(k) accounts to a brokerage IRA. Rollovers are tax-deferred and give you more control over your retirement funds while also providing much greater flexibility and opportunities for diversification.

In addition, if you have worked for several employers, the rollover to a brokerage IRA allows you to pull together.

PAYOUT USING 4% RULE

Multiple 401(k)'s for ease of record keeping. Talk to your tax advisor.

Financial advisors and planners highly recommend the payout of principal and income using the 4% rule. In this method, the retiree withdraws 4% of the account value at the beginning of each year and parks the money in a money market account, savings account or short-term government bond fund. This money is then divided up over 12 months for income. The remaining principal is allowed to grow over the next twelve months. All dividends and interest are reinvested. At the start of the next year, 4% is removed from the account and set aside in cash for the next year.

This 4% withdrawal technique works very well in a rising market. In the following pages, I have illustrated two payouts using S&P 500 Index stock returns over the periods from 1994 to 2024 and from 2000 to 2024. In both of these periods of time, the returns were very good long-term. However, note that in years of a declining market, your income would have dropped. Also, in a prolonged downturn in the market, as you sell shares for income, you could deplete your principal.

Remember, Warren Buffett often warns investors that if you cannot stand a 50% drop in your portfolio, you should not invest.

The average 401(k) balance that I have seen cited by Vanguard is $272,000. Therefore, this is the amount that I used in the following calculations. The S&P 500 returns are from Slickcharts.com. Calculations were done on the Texas Instruments BA Business Analysts Calculator. Note that the returns shown in the following illustrations are from the S&P 500 Index. You cannot invest in an index, but you can invest in one of the exchange-traded funds (ETFs) that are invested in the S&P 500 stocks.

S&P 500 Returns on a Hypothetical Investment of $272,000 Over 30 Years 1994-2024 With 4% Annual Withdrawals and all Dividends Reinvested.

Financial Data

Year	Value start of yr.	4% withdrawal.	Gain or loss.	Value end of the year
1994	$272000	$10880	1.32%	$257673
1995	$257673	$10306	37.58%	$340326
1996	$340326	$13613	22.96%	$401726
1997	$401726	$16069	33.36%	$514312
1998	$514312	$20572	28.58%	$634851
1999	$634851	$25394	21.04%	$737687
2000	$737687	$29507	-9.1%	$643735
2001	$643735	$25749	-11.89%	$544507
2002	$544507	$21780	-22.1%	$407204
2003	$407204	$16288	28.68%	$503030
2004	$503030	$20121	10.88%	$430369
2005	$430369	$17214	4.91%	$433440
2006	$433440	$17337	15.79%	$481805
2007	$481805	$19272	5.49%	$487926
2008	$487927	$19517	-37%	$295097
2009	$295097	$11803	26.46%	$358253
2010	$358253	$14330	15.06%	$395717
2011	$395717	$15828	2.11%	$387904
2012	$387904	$15516	16%	$431970
2013	$431970	$17278	32.39%	$549010
2014	$549010	$21960	13.69%	$599203
2015	$599203	$23968	1.38%	$583173
2016	$583173	$23326	11.96%	$626804
2017	$626804	$25072	21.83%	$733090
2018	$733090	$29323	-4.38%	$672941
2019	$672941	$26917	31.49%	$849457
2020	$849457	$33978	18.4%	$965526

2021	$965526	$38621	28.71%	$1193020
2022	$1093020	$47720	-18.11%	$937885
2023	$937885	$37515	26.29%	$1137077
2024	$1137077	$45483	25.55%	$1370497

As you read this chart, you can see that the principal grew from $272,000 in 1994 to $ 1,370,497 in 2024. This is great. However, there were several years in which the values declined, and hence, withdrawing 4% of the lower amount meant that the retiree would have received less income. There were six years out of thirty in which a market decline brought about a reduction in income. The worst cut in income came in 2007-2008 when income dropped from $19,517 to $11,803. This is an $8,000 reduction in income. Ask yourself if you could withstand an $8,000 cut in retirement income.

In the next chart, we will look at a shorter period. In this chart, we examine the S&P 500 Index from 2000 to 2024. The withdrawal percentage is the same 4% at the beginning of each year, with all dividends reinvested.

Financial Data 2000-2024

Year	Value at start of year	4% withdrawal	Gain/loss	Value year end
2000	$272,000	$10,880	-9.10%	$237,358
2001	$237,358	$9,494	-11.89%	$227,863
2002	$227,863	$9,114	-22.10%	$170,405
2003	$170,405	$6,816	28.68%	$210,506
2004	$210,506	$8,420	10.88%	$224,072
2005	$224,072	$8,962	4.91%	$225,671
2006	$225,671	$9,026	15.79%	$250,852
2007	$250,852	$10,034	5.49%	$254,039
2008	$254,039	$10,161	-37.00%	$153,642

2009	$153,642	$6,145	26.46%	$186,524
2010	$186,524	$7,461	15.06%	$206,030
2011	$206,030	$8,241	2.11%	$201,962
2012	$201,962	$8,078	16.00%	$224,904
2013	$224,904	$8,996	32.39%	$285,841
2014	$285,841	$11,433	13.69%	$311,974
2015	$311,974	$12,478	1.38%	$303,628
2016	$303,628	$12,145	11.96%	$326,344
2017	$326,344	$13,053	21.83%	$381,682
2018	$381,682	$15,267	-4.38%	$350,365
2019	$350,365	$14,014	31.49%	$442,268
2020	$442,268	$17,690	18.14%	$502,699
2021	$502,699	$20,108	28.71%	$621,144
2022	$621,144	$24,845	-18.11%	$488,308
2023	$488,308	$19,532	26.29%	$592,017
2024	$592,017	$23,680	25.55%	$713,546

In this illustration, the principal again grew substantially. From $272,000 in 2000, the account increased to $713,546 in 2024. I did this while 4% was withdrawn each year. Again, note that in six of the years, the income decreased.

Check the Internet and the books listed in the last section of this book for index-based exchange-traded funds. The most commonly used ETFs are those based on the Standard & Poor's 500. You might also add an international or global ETF, such as one based on the Russell 2000. Again, check the fund Fact Sheet on the web for average annual returns and dividend yields.

INVESTING FOR DIVIDEND GROWTH

In the last chapter, we looked at an investment in which we kept reinvesting dividends each year and withdrew 4% of the value at the start of a new year. This allowed the growth of the principal but forced the investor to take a reduced income in those years when the market declined.

In this chapter, we will discuss investing for dividend increases.

About 600 stocks have a history of increasing their dividends. This means that if you bought these stocks and held them for the long term, your income would have grown without selling any shares and without worrying about market fluctuations.

Remember, dividends are not guaranteed and can be reduced or even eliminated if the company encounters financial problems.

Sources of information about companies that have increased their dividend include Mergen's Dividend Achievers and David Fish's website, Dividend Champions, Contenders, and Challengers. Dividend champions are those companies that have increased their dividends for 25 years or more. Dividend contenders have increased their dividends for 10 years to 24 years. Dividend challengers have increased their dividends for up to 9 years. See David Fish's website, "Dividend Champions, Contenders, and Challengers." This list shows the company, current dividend yield, recent dividend increase, and average increase for 1, 3, 5, and 10 years.

Other places for researching stocks include Seeking Alpha.com, Stock Analysis.com, and company annual reports. When analyzing stocks, keep in mind that you are looking for dividend yield. Do not confuse this with current return or total return, since the latter includes increased capital gain. When looking for income, look for current yield or dividend yield.

Also, do not buy stocks with very high yields, such as 12 or 14%. Such high yields could indicate that the company is paying out too much cash and could be in danger of cutting the dividend if things go bad. Look for free cash flow and payout ratio. It is generally recommended that investors stick with stocks with a payout ratio of 50% or less. Of course, there are some very well-established companies paying out 60% or 70% of free cash as dividends.

One of the best ways to build a portfolio of stocks with increasing dividends is to use exchange-traded funds. These funds are usually tied to an index and pay out dividends monthly or quarterly. Many of the major mutual fund companies offer exchange-traded funds. You can find details about these funds in Morningstar, Stockanalysis.com, and in the fund fact sheet. When researching exchange-traded funds, check the fund fact sheet for dividend yield or 30-day SEC dividend yield. The following are some exchange-traded funds (ETFs) that have attractive dividend yields and that invest in stocks with increasing dividends.

Dividend Funds Information

Fund	Ticker symbol	# holdings	Div. Yield	Payout ratio
Pro Share S&P 500 Div. Aristocrats	NOBL	66	2.04%	46.03%
ProSharea S&P Mid Cap 400	REGL	48	2.60%	N/A
Pro shares Russell 2000	SMDV	99	3.00%	50.32%
iShares	DGRO	406	2.30%	49.95%
Invesco High Yield Dividend Achievers	PEY	50	4.58%	67.40%
Invesco Dividend Achievers	PFM	419	1.60%	38.63%
Invesco International Div. Achievers	PID	44	3.50%	69.15%

The information listed above is from the fund fact sheets for the individual funds and stockanalysis.com. I make no guarantee or warranty on the accuracy of the information provided. This information changes daily. Check the fund fact sheets and stockanalysis.com, and the fund annual reports and prospectuses before investing money. There are no guarantees on any dividend or exchange-traded fund performance.

BONDS AND BOND FUNDS

For many years, investors and retirees invested in bank certificates of deposit and bonds for income in retirement. They made these investments based on the safety and guarantees of principal and income. However, with the housing market crash of 2007-2008, interest rates dropped so low that those seeking retirement income had to look elsewhere. Today, interest rates have rebounded but not to the degree that retirees enjoyed in the 1980s and 1990s. Furthermore, investment in bonds or certificates of deposit always locks you into a fixed income. Fixed interest rates, along with Social Security and defined benefit pension plans, meant that millions of retired people were living on a fixed income. However, it is understandable how retirees look to the safety of fixed interest rates and principal. In this section, we will look at bonds as a source of retirement income and discuss exchange-traded funds and mutual funds for greater diversification and flexibility.

Bond interest on an individual bond usually does not increase. The only exception to this is iBonds. Normally, if you buy a 20-year bond paying 4%, you are locked into 4% income for 20 years. Using your brokerage IRA, you can purchase individual bonds. For greatest safety, you can buy U.S. Treasury bonds. You can add some flexibility by building a bond ladder of bonds maturing at various intervals. However, doing so might lock you into some bonds with lower rates. Moreover, buying bonds subjects you to the interest rate risk and, with corporate bonds, the credit risk. Buying international bonds brings into play the currency risk. If you are buying U.S. Government bonds, you can do so through your brokerage IRA. If you are investing money outside of a retirement plan, you can make this investment by accessing TreasuryDirect.com.

In the following section, I provide a chart with some bond exchange-traded funds and some open-end mutual funds. The exchange-traded funds are usually the most flexible for trading and have the lowest cost. Check out the fund websites, annual reports, fact sheets, and prospectuses to become familiar with the risks. Remember, the treasury usually guarantees the U.S. Government bonds, but they still fluctuate in value on the market. In addition, the mutual funds and exchange-traded funds are not guaranteed and can fluctuate widely. Moreover, the interest payouts will change as bonds in the portfolios mature.

ETF and Mutual Funds Information

Fund	Ticker	Category	30 DAY SEC YIELD
iShares Core U.S. Gov. ETF	IFYB	1-5 years	3.87%
iShares U.S. gov. ETF	IEF	7-10 years	3.63%
iShares U.S Gov. ETF	GOVT	Diversified	3.25%
iShares U.S. Gov. ETF	TLT	20 yr. Bonds	4.74%
Vanguard Total Bond Market	BND	Domestic Investment grade	4.46%
Vanguard Total International Bd.	BNDF	International bond	3.19%
PIMCO Active Bond ETF	BOND	Diversified bonds	4.98%
Fidelity Total Bond Fund	FTBFX	Diversified bonds	4.42%

Remember, bonds and bond funds always fluctuate inversely to interest rates.

IMMEDIATE ANNUITIES

If you are looking for guaranteed income from some or all of your retirement funds, think about an immediate annuity. This annuity can provide for you or you and your spouse with a guaranteed lifetime income. The annuity is a contract in which you invest money and sign up for an income for your life or the lives of you and your spouse. If you take only a life income or a joint life income and you both die, that is the end of the money. Therefore, it is usually best to take a life income or a joint life income with 10 or 20 years certain. Under this type of contract, if you and your spouse select a joint life income with 20 years certain and you both die after 12 years, the remaining income is paid to your heirs for the remaining 8 years.

A good place to start is at immediateannuities.com. Go to this website and enter your age and sex, your spouse's age and sex, the amount of money to be invested, and your state. You will receive an illustration of a projected monthly income. From this, you can request more information about the various companies available and the projected revenue. Some companies also offer a cost-of-living rider, although that will mean a lower initial monthly income.

Be certain to check the investment grade of the various insurance companies. Standard and Poor's investment grade ratings are AAA, AA, A, and BBB. For Moody's, the investment grade ratings are Aaa, Aa, A, and Baa. For greater safety, select a company that is rated investment grade. Avoid insurance companies that are rated lower than BBB or Baa. Such companies are not investment grade. You can also check A.M. Best for more information on insurance companies. You can find the Best in your library. Also, if you work with an insurance agent, they might be able to recommend a good, sound insurance company for your annuity.

Here are some illustrations of joint life annuities from immediateannuities.com. These numbers are based on males and females, each age 65 and living in Illinois.

- $272,000 invested for a joint life annuity with 10 years certain: $1477 per month.
- $272,000 invested for a joint life income with 20 years certain: $1454 per month.

If we invest half of this amount into an annuity and invest the other half in one of the other techniques described above, here are the results:

- $136,000 in a joint life annuity with 10 years certain: $739 monthly.
- $136,000 in a joint life annuity with 20 years certain: $727 monthly.

Note: You will see on this website illustrations of Period Certain annuities. These are payouts over a specific number of years. For example, a 25-year period certain on $272,000 produces $1605 monthly for 25 years, and then it ends.

- $136,000 invested for 25 25-year period certain produces $803 per month for 25 years, and then it ends.

These Period Certain annuities produce more monthly income but are not life annuities. Therefore, investing in a Period Certain annuity produces the risk that you could run out of money.

Note about 403(b) plans: If you are a teacher or professor, or other employee of a non-profit organization, you might have a 403(b). If you do, and if it offers an annuity option, check out the life annuities available there.

Note about 401(k) plans: You can roll over your 401(k) money directly to an immediate annuity. Check with your tax advisor and read the IRS publications on rollovers.

THRIFT AND SAVINGS

I want to address thrift and savings in retirement. I mentioned at the beginning about writers who warn some retirees about saving too much. I noted that, while some people have substantial accumulation of retirement money, far too many have much smaller balances. For so many retirees and investors nearing retirement, thrift and savings will be important throughout their retirement years.

Contrary to what some advisors and writers suggest, saving money is necessary during retirement. Think about the car repairs, house repairs, and all of the other emergency expenses that you will encounter.

Savings should be the first outlay each month. Set aside cash first, not last, after your monthly expenses. You can ask your bank to establish a monthly transfer from your checking account to a savings account. Other places to park cash and emergency money are money market accounts, short-term certificates of deposit, and short-term government bond funds.

Another great place to park cash for emergencies and longer-term needs is U.S. Savings Bonds. You can establish an account with Treasury Direct and buy Series I bonds and Series EE bonds. The I bond pays interest that fluctuates with inflation. The EE bonds mature in 20 years and, if held to maturity, double the initial investment. Investing $100 in an EE bond buys a face amount of $200, which is the maturity amount. The EE bond receives additional interest for the last year to bring the average annual return to 3.5%. The limit on investment in either series is $10,000 per year.

Thrift should follow savings. Shopping at discount stores, cooking at home, raising a backyard vegetable garden, buying used cars, and downsizing your housing are all part of thrift and making your money last throughout retirement.

We enjoy visiting state parks. Here in Illinois, Indiana, and Kentucky, we have stayed at state parks with beautiful lodges, cabins, very reasonable dining rooms, swimming pools, and hiking trails. On these trips to state parks, I have often met frugal people.

In January and February, check the Amtrak website. Often in the winter, Amtrak sells a rail pass. The last one was ten rides for $300. This offers coach travel, but if you buy the pass and make your reservations, you can travel across the country. Just pack a bag with a blanket and some sandwiches. Find a hotel near your destination station that you can reach by walking or on public transportation.

Another cost-saving idea for travel is to find cruise ships offering discounted staterooms. These are unsold rooms on which the cruise line is offering deep discounts at the last minute.

SUMMARY

In this book, I have shown four techniques that produce retirement income while helping to preserve the principal and protect the income. I make no guarantees or warranties as to the information or the security of the investments. The income methods are as follows:

1. The 4% payout rule. Here you invest all or a part of your retirement money, reinvest all the dividends, and withdraw 4% of the account at the start of each year. The cash withdrawn each year is set aside in a cash account, money market account, or short-term government bond fund. This provides income for the year. The remainder of the account continues to grow and to fluctuate. This technique allows you to benefit from rising income as the account grows, but subjects you to declining income when the market falls.
2. Investing for dividend growth. Here you invest in stocks with a history of rising dividends, and you live off the dividends. The principal continues to grow; to rise and fall, but you are not withdrawing principal. The rising dividends provide your income. The best way to invest in the growth of dividend income is in index exchange-traded funds. These funds offer a diversified portfolio and assure you that if a stock ceases to increase its dividend, it is removed from the fund.
3. Bonds and bond funds. These bonds and bond funds offer steady income. You can invest in individual U.S. Government bonds for safety or in government and more diversified bond ETFs for greater diversification and potentially higher income.
4. Immediate annuities. These annuities offer life income and joint life income from an insurance company. The life incomes continue as long as you or your spouse is alive.
5. Thrift and savings. These are essential in protecting your income and providing an emergency reserve.

RECOMMENDED READINGS

A. David Bunsen, The Case for Dividend Growth.
B. Richard Evans, The Index Fund Book
C. Richard Ferri, All About Index Funds
D. Jason Fieber, The Dividend Mantra Way
E. Jason Fieber, Five Steps to Retire in Five Years
F. Benjamin Graham, The Intelligent Investor
G. David Schneider, Index Funds & ETFs: What they are and how to make them work for you
H. Jeremy Siegel, The Future for Investors: Why the Tried and the True Triumph Over the Bold and the New Michael Thompson, How to Invest in Index Funds Joseph Tigre and Joseph Lisanti, The Dividend Rich Investor: Building Wealth with High Quality Dividend Paying Stocks
I. Jeff Yeager, The Cheapskate Next Door
J. Jeff Yeager, How to Retire the Cheapskate Way.

www.ingramcontent.com/pod-product-compliance
Lightning Source LLC
LaVergne TN
LVHW050940210926
848482LV00013B/684
* 9 7 9 8 3 4 9 5 9 4 4 1 0 *